World Languages

Families in
Spanish

Daniel Nunn

Heinemann
LIBRARY
Chicago, Illinois

WITHDRAWN

© 2013 Heinemann Library
an imprint of Capstone Global Library, LLC
Chicago, Illinois

To contact Capstone Global Library please phone 800-747-4992, or visit our website www.capstonepub.com

All rights reserved. No part of this publication may be reproduced or transmitted in any form or by any means, electronic or mechanical, including photocopying, recording, taping, or any information storage and retrieval system, without permission in writing from the publisher.

Edited by Daniel Nunn, Rebecca Rissman & Sian Smith
Designed by Joanna Hinton-Malivoire
Picture research by Tracy Cummins
Production by Victoria Fitzgerald
Originated by Capstone Global Library Ltd
Printed and bound in the United States of America in North Mankato, Minnesota.
032013   007268RP

16 15 14 13
10 9 8 7 6 5 4 3

Library of Congress Cataloging-in-Publication Data
Nunn, Daniel.
  Families in Spanish : las familias / Daniel Nunn.
     p. cm.—(World languages - Families)
  Text in English and Spanish.
  Includes bibliographical references and index.
  ISBN 978-1-4329-7173-1—ISBN 978-1-4329-7180-9 (pbk.) 1. Spanish language—Textbooks for foreign speakers—English—
Juvenile literature. 2. Families—Juvenile literature. I. Title.

PC4129.E5N87 2013
468.2'421—dc23   2012020429

Acknowledgments
We would like to thank the following for permission to reproduce photographs: Shutterstock pp.4 (Catalin Petolea), 5 (optimarc), 5, 6 (Petrenko Andriy), 5, 7 (Tyler Olson), 5, 8 (Andrey Shadrin), 9 (Erika Cross), 10 (Alena Brozova), 5, 11 (Maxim Petrichuk), 12 (auremar), 13 (Mika Heittola), 5, 14, 15 (Alexander Raths), 5, 16 (Samuel Borges), 17 (Vitalii Nesterchuk), 18 (pat138241), 19 (Fotokostic), 20 (Cheryl Casey), 21 (spotmatik).

Cover photographs of two women and a man reproduced with permission of Shutterstock (Yuri Arcurs). Cover photograph of a girl reproduced with permission of istockphoto (© Sean Lockes). Back cover photograph of a girl reproduced with permission of Shutterstock (Erika Cross).

We would like to thank Rebeca Otazua Bideganeta for her invaluable help in the preparation of this book.

Every effort has been made to contact copyright holders of any material reproduced in this book. Any omissions will be rectified in subsequent printings if notice is given to the publisher.

Contents

¡Hola!

Me llamo Daniel.

Y ésta es mi familia.

Mi madre y mi padre

Ésta es mi madre.

mi padre

Éste es mi padre.

Mi hermano y mi hermana

mi hermano

Éste es mi hermano.

Ésta es mi hermana.

Mi madrastra y mi padrastro

mi madrastra

Ésta es mi madrastra.

Éste es mi padrastro.

Mi hermanastro y mi hermanastra

mi hermanastro

Éste es mi hermanastro.

mi hermanastra

Ésta es mi hermanastra.

Mi abuela y mi abuelo

mi abuela

Ésta es mi abuela.

mi abuelo

Éste es mi abuelo.

Mi tía y mi tío

mi tía

Ésta es mi tía.

Éste es mi tío.

Mis primos

mi prima

Éstos son mis primos.

mi primo

19

Mis amigos

mi amiga

Éstos son mis amigos.

mi amigo

21

Dictionary

Spanish Word	How To Say It	English Word
abuela	a-bue-la	grandmother
abuelo	a-bue-lo	grandfather
amiga	a-mee-ga	friend (female)
amigo	a-mee-go	friend (male)
amigos	a-mee-gos	friends
es	es	is
ésta	es-ta	this (female)
éste	es-te	this (male)
éstos	es-tos	these
familia	fa-mee-lee-a	family
hermana	er-maa-na	sister
hermanastra	er-maa-nas-tra	stepsister
hermanastro	er-maa-nas-tro	stepbrother
hermano	er-maa-no	brother
hola	o-la	hello
madrastra	maa-dras-tra	stepmother

Spanish Word	How To Say It	English Word
madre	maa-dre	mother
me llamo	me ya-mo	my name is
mi	mee	my (singular)
mis	mees	my (plural)
padrastro	paa-dras-tro	stepfather
padre	paa-dre	father
prima	pree-ma	cousin (female)
primo	pree-mo	cousin (male)
primos	pree-mos	cousins
son	sohn	are
tía	tee-a	aunt
tío	tee-o	uncle
y	ee	and

See words in the "How To Say It" columns for a rough guide to pronunciations.

Index

Notes for Parents and Teachers

In Spanish, nouns are either masculine or feminine. The word for "this" changes accordingly—either *éste* (masculine) or *ésta* (feminine). The Spanish word for "these" used on pages 18 and 20 is *éstos*, which is the masculine plural. The feminine plural used to describe two or more female cousins or friends would be *éstas*.

Sometimes nouns have different spellings, too. This is why the word for "cousin" can be spelled either *primo* (male) or *prima* (female), and the word for "friend" can be spelled either *amigo* or *amiga*. The masculine plurals *primos* and *amigos* are used to describe a mixed group. The feminine plurals used to decribe female cousins or friends would be *primas* or *amigas*.

24

31901055110094